How To Keep Your Man

Darren G. Burton

This paperback edition 2012

ISBN 978-1477565858

Front Cover Photography: Paul Parzych
Cover Design: Darren G. Burton

ABOUT THE AUTHOR

Born in Sydney, Australia, Darren G. Burton has been writing for more than 20 years. He has had numerous articles and short stories published in major Australian publications and has written several full-length novels. With a keen interest in the arts, his other artistic pursuits include electric guitar and songwriting, creating ambient music CDs, photography and landscape painting.

This book is dedicated to all those who seek long-lasting happiness and fulfillment.

'Love: The irresistible desire to be irresistibly desired.'
Mark Twain

'Real love stories never have endings.'
Richard Bach

'Love doesn't make the world go round.
Love is what makes the ride worthwhile.'
Franklin P. Jones

'You don't love a woman because she is beautiful,
but she is beautiful because you love her.'
Anonymous

'Love is grand; divorce is a hundred grand.'
Unknown

Acknowledgements

The author would like to extend his heartfelt gratitude to all those who have generously contributed to this book. To those who participated in surveys and interviews, family and friends, and to my fiancé, Michelle, for her input and continued support.

Contents

Foreword

This book has been written from information gathered through conducting numerous surveys and interviews; men being the particular focus, but women have offered their viewpoints as well. Added to the mix is some common knowledge learnt over time and the author's own personal experiences.

No material in this book is meant to be offensive in any way. The advice and information on offer can either be taken on board to produce positive results in your life, or ignored if you so choose.

The author has made every attempt to write the book in an objective and unbiased manner, but it should be noted that it is virtually impossible to convey any information and points of view without any bias present whatsoever.

The information in this book is somewhat general in nature, and the author acknowledges the fact that individuals and personal circumstances vary.

The author is assuming that you are with a man (or plan to attract a man) who is worth keeping. The advice contained in this text is not designed to turn an incompatible partner into a compatible one; although even this situation can be vastly improved.

Whilst this text is predominantly aimed at women, it can certainly be enjoyed by men as well.

Introduction

Much has been written about how to attract a man. But once you have your man, how do you keep him?

Why do some men stray while others are loyal? Does it all come down to a man's intrinsic personality and character, or do other factors contribute?

From a man's perspective (and the same applies equally in reverse) there are things women do in a relationship that can drive a wedge between a couple. On the positive side, there are many things a woman can do in a relationship that will stoke the fires of our passion for them, fill us with contentment and joy, and keep us by our woman's side forever. Not just keep us there, but keep us wanting to be there.

And that is the purpose of this book: To let women know, from the male perspective, what it is that has the potential to drive us away and, more significantly, what it is that keeps us happy and contented with the woman we love.

Communication

Communication has been dealt with first, because without effective communication between you and your partner your relationship will eventually be doomed. Everything else that's good in the relationship will ultimately suffer if the channels of communication are not open.

Unfortunately, we men aren't the mind readers many women seem to think and hope that we are. We are just not that gifted. More often than not we need to be told things, straight up and in plain English, for us to get the message and for it to sink in.

Talk To Us

If something is on your mind, tell us. Don't just walk around presuming our powerful intuition will naturally kick in and we'll tune into the signals. We may pick up on the vibe, but we won't know exactly what it is. The chances of a light clicking on in our minds and the inner voice saying, "Ah ha, I know what it is," are very slim.

Once you have decided to talk to your man about something that is on your mind, you then have to decide on the best possible approach bring it up. This will depend on several factors.

- The nature of the subject
- Your mood and his
- The temperament of your partner

If the subject of your discussion or concern is of a sensitive nature, particularly for him, then you will have to choose your timing and words very carefully. Maybe even run it by a close friend first - preferably one who knows both you and your partner - what it is you want to say to your man, just in case it sounds like it might be coming out all wrong, or could be misinterpreted.

If you are upset about something, or angry, try to refrain from announcing the issue while in this frame of mind. Approaching your man when you are angry will more than likely just lead to an argument. If a man feels like he is being verbally attacked (or is about to be) he will naturally go into defensive mode to repel that attack, and anything on your mind that you want to convey will either come out all wrong, or the problem will just be exacerbated. Likewise, if he is in a negative or moody mindset, wait until his mood is lighter before approaching him.

Every man varies, as we all know, and that also applies to one's temperament. Some men are very calm and relaxed, even in the face of adversity. Others are angered easily. Only you know the temperament of your man. Always keep that in mind when bringing up any sort of touchy subject and act accordingly.

Be A Good Listener

Generally speaking women like to talk more than men. It's just a part of a woman's make up. However, men need to talk and express themselves as well.

Sometimes your man will need to vent about the happenings of the day. Or he may have something on his mind that he just needs to get off his chest or bounce off of you.

Be a good listener. Be attentive. Even if you don't particularly want to hear about his day at work or whatever, take the time out to listen to him anyway. You don't necessarily need to comment or offer an opinion. Just listen, be genuinely sympathetic or empathetic and let him know that you are always there for him if he needs to speak his mind.

Male or female, we all need to know that our partner is there for us in every way, and that they will always have an attentive ear if we need to talk.

Feedback and Input

If you are with a man who never seeks your input nor respects your feedback, or a man who constantly ridicules you for your feedback and input, then he is not the kind of man you want to keep. Hopefully most readers are not with an egotistical, insensitive brute like that.

A regular guy genuinely enjoys and respects feedback from the woman in his life. If he's smart he'll realise that he actually needs it. We all have our strengths and weaknesses, male or female, and there are always certain insights a woman can offer a situation that a man just won't see.

Real men want you to express your views on things, to tell them honestly what you think. Whether your man agrees with what you have to say or not is irrelevant. The important thing is that you are showing an interest in something he is doing, is planning on doing, or is interested in. If you really don't like something he's made, for example, try to be tactful in saying so. Maybe offer some tips for improvement? If the feedback has some positive element or angle attached to it, it will almost always be well received.

Any man worth being with will relish feedback and input from his partner.

Expectations

The word 'expectations' can be a positive one or a negative one. Having unrealistic expectations in our lives can lead to intense frustration and unhappiness. Having expectations that are set too low could mean we don't achieve a level of happiness and fulfillment that we are capable of achieving for ourselves.

It's all about balance and being realistic.

What are your expectations of your relationship? And what expectations do you have of, or place upon, your man?

If your partner is regularly having unrealistic expectations placed upon him, particularly ones that he just isn't capable of living up to, he is going to grow frustrated; becoming disillusioned and aloof, depressed and negative. Ultimately he will blame you for the way he is feeling because he can't live up to what it is you are asking of him. If things can't be resolved, he will eventually want to end the relationship and move on.

It is vitally important to have realistic expectations of yourself, your relationship and your partner. We all have our gifts and we all have our limitations. Some of the weaker areas can be improved upon. Some cannot, or can be improved only marginally. There is no point expecting your man, if he is a woeful singer for example, to be able to improve his voice to the point where he becomes a Pavarotti.

Now this analogy may seem a little silly and extreme, but it is an example of having an unrealistic expectation; a goal that is fruitless and impossible. I think we've all been guilty of placing unattainable expectations upon ourselves and others.

It is imperative to communicate your goals together as a couple.

- What you expect of yourself
- What you expect of your partner
- What you expect from the relationship

'Communicate' is the operative word here: The key. Work out your goals together. Discuss them at length. Make sure that they are both achievable and realistic.

You can't expect your man to be something that he is either incapable of becoming, or is not interested in becoming. Respect him for who he is and what he wants and does. After all, you chose him for who he is in the first place. Why expect him to transform himself into something or someone else? It's not a fair thing to ask of anyone.

Secrets and Things Not Revealed

The subject of secrets can be a tricky one to deal with. Within a relationship there are two kinds of secrets, or undisclosed happenings.

- Events that occurred prior to the relationship existing
- Things that have happened during the course of the relationship

It is true that some things that have happened in the past should be left in the past. After all, they are history. Why bring up an event that happened prior to the relationship that may create ill feeling between you and your partner? It serves no real purpose.

However, it is an entirely different story when it involves something that has happened throughout the course of the current relationship. Keeping secrets of this kind from your man can lead to major drama if he ever finds out about them. Honesty and openness prevail here, regardless of the outcome. Keeping your partner in the dark about something that has a direct bearing and impact on the relationship is a major breach of trust. And a relationship without trust and honesty is worth nothing.

Even if you refuse to tell him and he never finds out, guilt will eventually drive a wedge between you and ultimately lead to a possible break up.

The old adage of what 'someone doesn't know won't hurt' doesn't realistically work in this situation. Eventually it will have some affect on the relationship and ultimately it will hurt someone, in one way or another.

If your relationship with your man is an open and honest one, one built on trust, then there will never be cause to keep something from him as there will probably never arise the need to do so.

Disagreements and Arguments

It takes two to argue. No one can argue by themselves (not unless there are a few screws loose, maybe). There is also usually fault on both sides throughout the course of an argument or disagreement.

I'm not here to place blame on anyone, or to delve into the nitty gritty of arguments and disagreements. What I aim to offer in this section, based on my research, is some insight into what women will sometimes inadvertently do during an argument that can frustrate her male partner and cause the argument to escalate.

Men, on the whole, are not overly emotional creatures. However, we do tend to be more assertive and aggressive and can usually be angered more easily, in certain circumstances, than women. We also tend to have less patience and a reduced level of tolerance. On the flipside though, due to our innate lack of intense emotions, we can be cruisy and easy going in most everyday situations. There are many things that will bother a woman, or seem like a big deal to her, that will not affect a man anywhere near as deeply.

This is the first point women need to grasp. You can't hold a man accountable for not feeling as deeply or strongly about something emotional as you do. We just aren't wired to feel things as acutely. It's a scientific fact.

Second, due to this difference in inherent emotional depth, men are often left confused and shaking their heads when confronted by their partner exasperated by something that he either doesn't see (or feel) is a big deal, or plain just doesn't comprehend what all the fuss is over. When men can't fathom confrontations of this nature, when they have no 'logical' answer to it all, they then tend to become extremely frustrated and then angry.

From this point on the argument can escalate into something really ugly.

There is no easy answer or solution to this dilemma. Men can't expect women to be as logical as them any more than women can expect men to be more emotional.

What you can do though, in these types of situations, is try to keep your emotions under control as much as possible. If you feel things are getting out of hand, walk away, take in some deep breaths and try to be calm.

This is the secret. The calmer you are, emotional or not, the more *logical* your words will seem to your partner. If you speak in a tone built purely on hyped up emotions, your man will instantly switch into defensive mode to repel what he will see as nothing more than the emotional rantings of a female.

As much as women may wish we could, we men just can't relate to that. It's not intrinsic in our nature.

The best solution, as hard as it may be, is to always remain calm. Speak your mind, endeavour to get your point across about how you are feeling, but do it positively and placidly.

I assure you, you'll be amazed at the instant and encouraging results.

PMS

A touchy subject.

Every man alive dreads this stage of the month. Most of the time we don't even know it is happening until it's in full swing. It doesn't dawn on us until well into the premenstrual stress cycle that this is why our girl is seemingly moodier and more acutely emotional and sensitive than normal.

How to help us poor men deal with this time of the month?

Stay away from us!

I don't mean that to sound really harsh, but it is probably the best solution. A man can't really be of any significant help to a woman when she is in this phase. His mere presence or attempts at being understanding will probably just aggravate her anyway.

It's best all round if she keeps to herself and he stays the hell out of her way.

Compliments and Positive Affirmations

Women thrive on genuine compliments. That's a well known fact. Men prosper from positive affirmations as well, despite our apparent lack of emotion.

No compliment holds more meaning to a man than genuine positive words spoken either to him, or about him, from the lips of the woman he loves.

Men need to know that the way they look, the way they are, or the things they do please their partner. It is an essential and sometimes underrated element in a man's personal growth and the bonding process between man and woman.

Give compliments to your man freely and regularly, and be genuine about them. Above all, never offer a compliment with the sole desire of hoping to receive one in return.

Offer your words of praise unconditionally.

Notes and Messages

Small gestures can mean a lot. Often it's the little things that can speak volumes about how you feel towards your partner. There are many different forms of communication, and one of the simplest and most effective ways to express terms of endearment is through little notes and messages.

It's just yet another way to show you are thinking about him.

If he takes a packed lunch to work, every now and then slip a little surprise note in with it. It doesn't really matter what the note says, so long as it's something positive. The note might just say something simple like:

- I love you
- Thinking of you
- You are the world's sexiest man

It doesn't take much to have a uplifting effect.

Modern technology provides other easy means of achieving the same result. Fire him up by sending him a saucy text message on his phone, telling him what you plan to do to him when he gets home that night. Or send a message of thanks and appreciation for something he might have done around the house recently.

If he works on a computer and you have access to the internet, send him a brief email. Maybe even include a sexy picture of yourself?

These little messages, small snippets of thoughts, feelings and appreciation can work wonders in a relationship. And they are so easy to do, cost virtually nothing and can be done on a regular basis. Don't do it all the time so it becomes mundane and loses some of its meaning and impact. But surprise him regularly with different little messages and he will love you for it.

At the very least it will put a smile on both of your faces.

Giving and Receiving

Are you a giver, or are you a receiver?

Actually, you need to be both.

Men generally enjoy giving to the lady in their life, especially gifts and flowers and little surprises. If he doesn't, it does not necessarily mean he doesn't love you. He might just not be thinking of you as much as he should be. If that is the case, you may need to look at the reasons why. Maybe he's just been very snowed under with work? Or there have been a lot of other things cluttering his mind?

In any case, that doesn't mean that *you* can't be a giver.

Men like to receive little surprises as well. A gift or surprise doesn't have to be anything costly either. In fact, some of the most cherished gifts are those that have been made or created personally by the giver.

Surprises and gifts, small gestures of thoughtfulness, are often best offered when the recipient least expects it.

We all know we are going to give and receive gifts on birthdays, Christmas and the like. Often we feel like it is mandatory to do so. Giving gifts on these occasions, although still nice but often expected, does not have nearly the same impact as a surprise when there is no actual reason for the surprise, other than that you *really wanted to do it.*

Although it shouldn't be the sole purpose for giving, as giving should predominantly be from the heart, these acts of selflessness could lead to your man paying more attention to you and your needs, thinking about you more throughout the day, and possibly coming home from work with a surprise that you didn't expect.

You also need to know how to receive graciously as well. Even if you don't really like his gift, be appreciative of the thought and heart attitude behind it.

That is what's important.

Tell Him You Love Him

Men like to hear those three magic words almost as much as women do.

"I love you."

As much as this phrase is commonly used, I don't think they are words that can ever be overdone, overstated or overused.

Don't always wait for your partner to say it first. Take the initiative. Tell him, and tell him regularly.

We all know when we're loved. It shows through in a person's actions and attitude toward us. And actions speak volumes. But that aside, we all still need to hear those words actually voiced; and often.

Personality and Character

Understanding your man - his ways, his moods, why he is the way he is - is essential for a successful, fulfilling and long lasting relationship between the two of you. Learning about your partner takes time and patience and some effort on your part, but it is a richly rewarding experience, and one that will even help you to learn more about yourself.

This section of the book is not just about your man, his personality and character, but also about your own make up, your attitudes and the way you are toward him and your relationship.

His Personality

A simple definition of personality is this: The way we express ourselves. Every one of us is an individual and no two personalities are exactly the same.

Never, ever seek to change your man's personality! After all, the way he comes across, the manner in which he expresses himself, had a lot to do with why you were attracted to him in the first place and why you fell for him.

The only exception to this is if a man was pretending to be someone that he truly wasn't, just to lure you in. If that is the case, and I sincerely hope that it is not, then it would be a good time to rethink whether you want to be with a man who has no apparent qualms about deceiving you like that.

Another important point to remember is to never compare him to a past love. Everyone hates that.

As stated earlier, take the time to get to know your partner. Appreciate him for the way he is. Encourage him to be himself and learn to grow with each other.

His Character

Character is not the same as personality, although it does affect one's personality. Essentially and in simple terms, character is what we are made of. Some elements of character include, but are in no way limited to:

- Our morals and beliefs
- How we deal with things
- Strengths and weaknesses in our psychological profile
- Our code of conduct
- Our sense of right and wrong

Your partner's character, or anyone's for that matter, will only be revealed over the course of time. And chances are, you could spend a lifetime with the one person and still not know everything about them. It virtually takes a lifetime to get to truly know ourselves let alone someone else.

Character is deep, character is ingrained, and it has many, many layers.

Because character traits can be so ingrained into a person's make up, they can be very difficult to change in the case of a character flaw.

We'll be dealing with the subject of character flaws in the next section of this book. For now I just wanted to express the difference between personality and character in general.

As a closing point for now, encourage your man to exhibit and revel in those character traits that you have learned to recognise in him as strengths.

Trust

Do you trust your man? Does he trust you? Is there an underlying element and sense of trust in your relationship in general?

If there is not, then you have major problems.

No relationship can survive without trust permeating the entire union. It is the foundation upon which the bond between man and woman is built; an essential component of any important connection between two or more people.

If your partner doesn't trust you, do you give him a reason or reasons not to trust you? If you don't have faith in your man, is he doing something to make you feel this way?

Sometimes we don't trust someone simply out of fear. Afraid that they *might* do something. This kind of anti-trust borders on the irrational, but is also a normal part of the process in growing to trust someone. And it is a growth phase. We don't automatically trust another person until we get to know them better. Until we reach that point of familiarity it's more a benefit-of-the-doubt situation.

Show your man that you trust him; especially when you are apart. If he has given you no reason to doubt him, don't assume he is up to no good, or accuse him of anything of which there is no logical or rational proof. Go with the flow and naturally, over time, let him prove himself to you without prejudice or judgement.

If a situation does arise where he has breached your trust, deal with the issue then. At least, through your initial faith in him, you didn't do anything to contribute to the situation or cause it to happen.

Let me elaborate on that point. A fact that came to light in the surveys was that some men felt almost driven to do the wrong thing, in one form or another, because their partner didn't trust them to begin with. Some men were constantly being accused of things they simply hadn't done. A few of them, in the end, decided to actually do the things they were being accused of, because they were constantly being accused of them anyway.

Never allow yourself to fall into this trap.

You can never control what your partner does, but you do have total control over what you do.

Therefore, be trustworthy yourself. Never give your partner a reason to doubt your trustworthiness or faithfulness. Any man of solid character and true love for you will be loyal to you forever if treated the right way.

Loyalty

Loyalty, the act of being faithful, steadfast and trustworthy, sometimes beyond the point of logical reason, can exist for many reasons.

- An inherent character trait
- Being treated the right way
- Having one's needs met
- Showing faith in a person
- Treating one with respect
- Being loved

These are just some of the more general reasons why a person may be loyal. The list, in reality, is probably endless.

Having someone's undying loyalty is one of the greatest blessings any partner can hope to have in a relationship. As stated in the previous topic, loyalty often goes hand in hand with trust. Unless your man has flawed character, treat him the right way as much as you possibly can, and you will have a loyal life partner. And be a loyal partner yourself, as it's very difficult to remain loyal to a person who doesn't reciprocate.

Be Supportive

Your guy needs to know that you are supportive. It is something a man really relies on and thrives on within a relationship. If your support wavers, is inconsistent, or doesn't exist at all, these are all factors that can really play with a man's mind and ultimately his direction and motivation.

Every man interviewed, surveyed, every man I've ever known, including myself, all stressed that the support of their partner in life's endeavours and pursuits is a vital and key element in the eventual success or failure of those pursuits.

When on our own, we men still pursue things.

- Careers
- Money
- Adventure
- Lifestyle

However, our attention can often be somewhat divided among going after these things, and seeking out a life partner.

Once in a loving relationship men can usually focus much better on the pursuit of careers and money and everything that comes with it. Sure, he still needs to pay attention to the lady in his life and nurture the relationship so it doesn't wilt and die, but he naturally finds himself being able to focus more on other ventures than he ever could before.

The reasons for this are simple. He now has two very important elements in his life fulfilled.

- Stability
- The support of a loving partner

Now, once in this coexisting situation, if the state of the union between himself and his girl becomes unstable in any way, or she refuses to, or is inconsistent in offering her support of his endeavours, a man suddenly finds it very hard, if not virtually impossible, to give a project (or a goal or dream) his one hundred percent commitment and effort.

That is why it is so vital for a woman to give her man complete support.

In some ways this support does come with conditions attached. If your partner is hell bent on pursuing some ludicrous, possibly dangerous or otherwise foolish goal, then it will prove very difficult for you to support him on it.

This is where your vital and much needed feedback and input really come into play. If his plans really aren't wise, and you are sure no good will come of it, stick to your guns, tell him why you think the way you do and that you can't offer support in such an endeavour.

On the other hand, if his plans seem solid, or you are just not sure about them one way or the other, give him your vote of confidence. Offer positive input and help him see things through to fruition.

Commitment

It is obvious that commitment is a very important component in a serious relationship. We all realise that. Without it the relationship is at best just a casual one (or just starting out).

Hopefully you and your partner are totally devoted to one another. But if there are commitment problems between you and your man, you have to ask yourself why.

- Is it you who is not one hundred percent committed?
- Does he maybe have some doubts?

Suffering a commitment problem is certainly not uncommon. Most of us have probably been through it to some degree at some stage in our lives; particularly early on in a relationship. Obviously, if a partnership is going to progress to the next level, then a solid commitment from both parties needs to come into play.

If you are suffering from an inability to commit to the man you are with, you need to work out why this is so. Maybe the answer is obvious? Possibly he's not the kind of man you feel comfortable wholeheartedly giving yourself to? If that is the case, and there are valid reasons for feeling the way you do, then he just might not be the right guy for you. If you can't come up with any obvious or logical reasons why, then possibly the problem lies within yourself and not with him?

Fear brought about by past bad experiences is a common reason for people struggling to commit. Although difficult, these fears from the past need to be put behind you so your current relationship doesn't suffer and has every chance to succeed. Sure, learn from your experiences and mistakes, but don't let the past ruin your future.

Maybe you are one hundred percent devoted to your man, but he is not reciprocating the same level of devotion? There may be a chance he is suffering from the *past experience syndrome*? Or he may be unsure of something about you?

If enough time has passed where you believe he should be committing but isn't, don't let it go on. You need to find out why.

Talk to him, tactfully and gently. Try to draw out the reasons, but never harass him about it. Men hate being badgered about emotional stuff, but we will confide in the reasons bit by bit over time.

Above all, have patience and give the 'drawing out the reasons why' process a little time. Once the reasons are revealed, it will then be a case of discussing possible solutions between the two of you. Only you and your partner will know how to resolve the commitment issue, depending on why the problem exists.

Complacency

Although not necessarily a major or immediate cause of break ups, complacency does have a way of dulling a relationship. What was once a passionate union of man and woman, raging like a house on fire, can end up as dreary and unsavoury as a smoldering ashtray.

We've all heard that relationships take work. They don't just happen. And they certainly don't remain hot and spicy without some conscious effort. None of us wants a boring and lifeless relationship, but many of us end up with exactly that over time.

A number of things, in fact many different things, can help us keep a relationship fired up. These include:

- Quality time
- Intimacy
- Having fun
- Escapism
- Variety
- Romance

These topics will be covered in more detail later on in the book. For the moment we will move on to the next topic, which deals with complacency toward your man specifically.

Don't Take Him For Granted

Men, as much as women, like to be appreciated. As covered earlier, men like compliments, need love and support, and a partner who is passionate about them as an individual, and passionate about their relationship together.

We are all probably guilty of this. Male or female, we all, at least on occasion, fall into the trap of taking our partner for granted.

Do you ever feel like this with your guy?

Stop and think for a moment. Does your mind ever harbour any of these thoughts?

- He'll always be there
- We'll have sex another time
- I don't need to tell him I love him, he knows I do
- He *should* buy me dinner, he's a man
- He knows I appreciate him

- It's his job to do that
- I don't have time to talk about this now

These types of thoughts, and they creep insidiously into all of our minds from time to time, are signs of taking someone for granted.

Remaining diligent in your relationship - being conscious of showing genuine appreciation, respect and gratitude – takes effort. And that's the answer right there. We get complacent, we take our partner for granted, we take our relationships for granted, because the alternative takes *effort*!

Think back to when you first met your partner; the excitement you felt, the thrill of the blossoming romance. Chances are you were constantly making a conscious effort to put your best foot forward, to please him as much as possible, thanking him for every little thing he did with warm hugs and passionate kisses.

Why should this change?

The only reason it changes is that, over time, we start to slacken off in our efforts. We have our partner now. It takes energy and effort to maintain that level of intense interaction and eagerness to please.

How do you know he'll always be there? We never know how much time we have. Live for the now. Enjoy the moment. Don't put off for tomorrow what you can do today.

It would be naive and somewhat unrealistic to suggest that any couple can maintain the level of passion and intensity first experienced at the start of, and during the early stages of the relationship. But we can make an effort in some way, every day, to keep the passion alive and eradicate boring routine.

Try and think of at least one thing you can do every single day to show your man that you love him and appreciate him. This will have a very positive affect on him. Positive actions produce positive reactions. Chances are, he'll start doing the same in return.

Nagging

Nagging is a dreaded word for most men, and a dreaded sound. In all honesty – and a fact backed up by the surveys and interviews with men, women and couples alike – nagging is one of the things men hate the most in a relationship. It's not an endearing quality.

I'm not here to say that all women on the planet are naggers, or that there is never any justifiable cause to nag. I'm just expressing the thoughts and feelings of the male population as a whole in saying that we men dislike it immensely.

Perhaps some men need to be nagged, or even deserve it? There are those that just wouldn't get anything done without their lady riding them. These types of men probably require the same kind of hounding from their bosses in their jobs as well. If you are dating or married to a man you feel you have to nag, then nagging is probably the only option open to you if he is inherently unmotivated. But remember, you chose this man. And you continue to choose to be with him.

If your partner *is* more motivated and usually gets the chores done, generally keeping on top of things, if you nag him every time you want something done, solved, resolved, then he is going to take offence to what he will see as a misguided attitude.

So what if he didn't do something exactly when you wanted him to? At least he does get around to it sooner rather than later.

Nine times out of ten nagging is a character flaw; an annoying and repetitive bad habit that needs to be monitored, addressed and brought under control. Nag too much and you might just hound your guy right out the door.

As alluded to in the *Communication* section earlier, there are more subtle and effective ways of getting your point across.

Who's The Boss?

- What is the balance of power in your relationship? Is there one?

- Are you in charge for the most part, or is he?
- Is there a constant power struggle?
- Do you evenly share the responsibilities of decision making? Does this Work?
- Is he dominant while you are submissive, or vice versa?

All very interesting questions.

Unfortunately, some couples can't even answer these questions. They have no idea of who's in charge of what and when. This type of indecisiveness can lead to serious problems down the track, issues that usually end up in major arguments.

In every association of any kind - whether it be business, sport, or personal relationships - there has to be some form of leadership and decision making process. How you orchestrate that in your relationship is up to you and your partner, but there has to be some leadership. Sometimes leadership sways toward the person with the more dominant personality and happens quite naturally.

Modern day couples tend to share this responsibility, with both the man and the woman having equal say. Frequently nowadays this is just an unspoken rule of engagement and is expected. This is fine so long as there is no confusion, and no unfair blame being placed on one another by each other.

Often it is a better idea to allocate who is in charge in what area, and who is primarily responsible for what.

Where children are involved the mother will generally take charge of the decisions regarding their day to day lives, while the father concerns himself more with the financial aspects of the family unit. Sometimes it's the other way around. However way you allocate duties, decision making and responsibilities in your relationship, make sure they are clear and defined, and that they are fair.

If you happen to be the dominant partner in your relationship, a little tip for you: Even though your man might be less dominant and more submissive than you are, give him the impression from time to time that he is in charge. Men like to feel that they are the boss. It's fundamentally embedded within our nature. Stroke his ego a little. It will work wonders.

Compatibility

Being compatible with your partner goes beyond just having some common interests. Many other aspects of ourselves as individuals come into the frame as well.

In this section we'll take a look at some of these so that you can not only understand and clarify where you and your man are compatible, but possibly identify areas or ways in which you can become even more compatible with your partner.

Common Ground

Having things in common is probably one of the main things that attracted you and your partner to each other.

Common interests - likes, dislikes, goals, ambitions and beliefs - are a very powerful magnet. It creates a feeling of empathy with one another and helps to generate that warm, fuzzy feeling and a sense of familiarity and closeness.

We all need to have things in common with our partner. Without mutual ground we'd just be too different and therefore distant. Even couples that seem like opposites, but gel well together, will still usually have things in common; and the differences between them will generally be complimentary ones.

Conflicting differences will cause exactly that: Conflict. Couples who are essentially incompatible or different in key areas won't stay together for long. Those discordant variances will soon drive them apart.

How many things do you have in common with your partner, and what are the differences?

An interesting exercise is to make a list of them. It will give you an idea of what works well for you and why, and what areas may cause issues between you and him.

Likes and Dislikes

To take this idea further, write out a general list of your likes and dislikes. The list might include things like:

- Music
- Movies
- Food
- Entertainment
- Fashion

Include whatever you want in your list. Create subheadings for each category. Under each subheading write down what you *do* like and what you *don't* like. When you have finished your list, write out another list in the exact same manner, but this time try to determine your partner's likes and dislikes in each category.

You'll discover two things during the course of this exercise. Firstly, you will determine just how well you do know your partner. Secondly, you may identify areas where there could be a source of contention, areas where you may have to learn to compromise.

Above all, try and respect your man for what he likes and dislikes. Never ridicule him for liking something just because you don't. After all, his interests are an integral part of him just as yours are a part of you. It is something that helps make us interesting.

Faults and Flaws

We all have them.

I'm not about to suggest you start writing out a list of your man's flaws. I believe this would be a negative process, and drawing undue attention to negatives doesn't really achieve much. However, you do need to be aware (as you probably already are) of the areas where he may be a little weaker in character and determine whether those areas could (or already do) present problems in your relationship.

If you have recognised something that is a problem, or a potential problem, then you need to figure out if it's a major or minor issue for you. If it's only minor, then just try to ignore it and live with it. If it's major, or has the potential to be so, you will need to tactfully try and work this out with your partner so that it doesn't lead to conflict and ill feelings.

This all comes back to communicating with him in a calm and rational manner. Remember, men respond much more favourably to logic than emotional outbursts. Always try to keep that in mind. It's imperative for a smooth relationship.

Another thing to always keep in mind is that you have flaws too, and you probably know what they are better than anyone. If he needs to discuss with you something that is bothering him about you, let him have his say and strive to be objective and calm in your response to his concerns.

We all have character flaws, but they can be fixed. It's difficult and it takes time, but it can be done with the right support, attitude and a little understanding of each other's differences.

Annoying Habits

Unfortunately we all suffer from these too.

We are unaware that our habits and little idiosyncrasies annoy others until they tell us. Obviously our own habits don't annoy ourselves or we would change them. And not everyone is the same either. What annoys one person may not bother another.

When living with someone – especially your partner where it's a lot more personal – a collection of small bothersome habits can culminate into one big problem. We have to learn to coexist in harmony.

If your guy has habits that annoy you, then there are basically only two courses of action open to you:

- You can try to ignore them and learn to live with them
- You can bring them to his attention and together try to work out a way to eradicate them completely, or at least lessen the problem

Once again I feel it necessary to emphasise the point that men detest being nagged. So that's definitely out as a means of knocking his habits on the head.

My fiancé put it well when I queried her on this point. She suggested that teaching a man to break a habit is much the same as training a child. I must admit, I wasn't overly enthused about the comment, but she's probably right. We men often are just like big kids.

Let him know that he does something that you find annoying, but don't be brutal about it. That kind of approach will just get his back up and he won't care about trying to change anything. If brought to his attention in the right manner, hopefully your man is considerate enough to take it on board and try to stop what it is he does that annoys you. He may struggle for a while. After all, it is a habit and they can be difficult to break.

Here's an example of something you can try that may help.

Let's say he has the old classic habit of leaving the lid off the toothpaste tube. He's trying to break the habit, but still forgets. You don't want to nag him about it, so you adopt an effective but more subtle approach. You leave a note under the toothpaste tube to remind him to replace the lid. This will serve to continually jog his memory and he'll soon get into the habit of putting the lid *back on.*

Another way to broach the topic of an annoying habit with your partner is to reciprocate in the deal. In other words, you can tell him one habit he has that you find annoying. Then he gets his turn to let you know of something you do that bothers him.

And always keep in mind that he won't be the only one in the relationship with annoying habits.

Temperament

Temperament, explained in simplistic terms, is a person's way of responding to the world. It is the integration of our personality and character combined and governs how we act and react, how motivated or aggressive we are etcetera.

We all vary in temperament, and a man's temperament is generally quite different to a woman's.

In order for a man and woman to get along in a life partnership, their respective temperaments need to have some key areas where they are similar, or differences that are complimentary.

It is going to be very hard for an extremely aggressive and motivated person to get along with a partner who is just as extremely laid back and placid. The two individuals just won't be on the same wavelength most of the time.

Conflicting differences in temperament can often be the cause of arguments and unrest in a relationship. We will never find a partner with whom we mesh with perfectly in every way and never disagree on anything. One of the keys to a successful partnership is to be with someone whose temperament is complimentary to your own, or at least both be willing to learn ways to compromise.

Tolerance and Understanding

These are probably the two most important elements to finding and maintaining that harmonious compatibility balance with your loved one.

Be tolerant of his differences and try to be understanding of who he is, and why he is the way he is.

Not one of us is exactly the same, and we wouldn't want it to be any other way. Life would be boring if we were all just clones of one another.

If you feel your man is not being tolerant and understanding of you and your needs, communicate this with him effectively. Let him know that it takes tolerance and understanding from both parties for you to get along and grow closer as a couple. Look for the good in the differences between the two of you and learn how you can combine the strengths of these differences to create an inseparable bond.

Quality Time

Every relationship needs quality time for the bond to remain close and to strengthen over time. Without quality time together a couple will gradually become distant and somewhat alienated from each other.

This section of the book is not just about spending quality time together. It's also about quality time for him.

Give Him Space

Men need time out to themselves: Time to reflect on the day, a moment to ponder, a chance to wind down. How much time your man needs and how often depends on his personality and temperament, and the circumstances of his life.

Perhaps his job is very physically and/or mentally demanding and draining. If that's the case, the very first thing he'll probably need at the end of a work day is some quiet time to himself for twenty minutes or so. This certainly isn't the right time of the day to hit him up with a problem, or to tell him what's on your mind. Greet him when he gets home, then let him be for half an hour.

Men also like to have an area of the house that is exclusively their domain (like the shed or garage).

We men need space at times for a number of reasons:

- To work out, in our own minds, a problem or an issue
- To ponder how to make more money
- To relax without anyone talking to us
- Unwind without any external stimuli (i.e. other people around, TV, music)

- Time out for hobbies and recreational pursuits
- Time to do guy stuff

Everyone needs time out to themselves, but men do especially. We are by nature more aggressive creatures and that all important chill out time allows us to unwind and prevents us from becoming agitated.

Make Time For Him

The modern world is often a busy and hectic one. Between work, chores, the children's needs, family and friends, there is often not much time left in the day. Next thing you know it's bed time, then the routine starts all over again from the moment you open your eyes in the morning.

It is very easy for a week or two to slip by in the blink of an eye and suddenly realise you've hardly spent any quality time with the man in your life.

In the previous topic we mentioned that your partner will need some quiet time to himself every so often. Help him to have that time, those moments of peace and serenity. Don't try to fill every waking moment of his day with things to do.

Likewise, in order to refresh your own mind and keep your sanity, you also need to allocate some quiet time alone for yourself as well. We all need this, at least in small doses.

Most of all though, make certain the two of you get some quality alone time together. Even if you can't be spontaneous about it and have to plan it, set aside a block of time at least once a week that is just for the two of you.

Which leads us onto the next topic.

Alone Time – Together

Having alone time together means exactly that: Alone. It doesn't involve socialising with friends, going to a family gathering, or spending time together in a crowded shopping mall. Although these things may be time out from work and chores and you are technically 'together', they defeat the purpose of this much required element of your relationship.

If it has to be planned or scheduled because of the constraints of everyday life then by all means plan it. If it can be spontaneous then all the better.

Spontaneity adds a touch of excitement to your time together. When something is totally unplanned and adlib things tend to be more of a surprise and therefore much more fun and interesting. Also, the moment flows naturally and nothing feels forced like can happen in some predetermined situations.

Don't always wait for your partner to organise some togetherness time. Planning something for him and yourself is fine, especially if he doesn't know about it and it's all a surprise.

Whatever you do together doesn't have to cost money either, or at least be relatively inexpensive.

Sharing a few glasses of good wine in the quiet hours of the night is a common and pleasant way to unwind together. The drop of alcohol also lends itself to freeing up the pair of you so that the moment and ensuing conversation flows in a relaxed manner.

Casually walking arm in arm on the beach or by the banks of a river or stream is great. It costs nothing to do and the presence and sound of water always has a calming influence.

A simple picnic on in a quiet area during a pleasant country drive is another good option. It gets you both out of the house and the routine. You add that little bit of adventure to the outing by not planning exactly where you are going to drive to, or where you are going to stop. A picnic also affords the opportunity to indulge in some relaxed and quality conversation. Who knows? You may even get intimate?

It doesn't really matter what you do so long as the time spent together in these special moments isn't interrupted or interspersed with the routines of your everyday lives.

Trips Away

These two words probably conjure up thoughts of expensive extended overseas holidays or vacationing around the country. If you and your partner can afford these types of trips (both in time and money) then by all means do it. Having adventures in lands abroad, exploring new places and cultures is a very rewarding experience, and the ensuing effects will flow positively through the fabric of your relationship.

With that said, trips away together don't have to be long ones or costly in monetary terms.

You could go camping for a weekend, or just get out of town for one night and spend an evening of uninterrupted passion in a motel somewhere.

The whole idea of the trip away someplace isn't just for the fun and excitement of it, it's also a ploy to force you and your partner out of your regular daily routines so you have no distractions and no intrusions on your quality time together.

Surprise your man occasionally. Book a night in a motel out of town and take him there. Have an uninhibited night of freedom and fun together. You don't even have to let on what you've got planned. Pack some things for the two of you, stow them in the car, then tell him you are taking him for a nice drive.

He'll be blown away when you arrive at your destination and he discovers what you have in store for him that night.

Men may not always say it, but we love it when our special lady does something totally unexpected and pleasant for us. It also inspires us to do the same.

Have A Laugh

Sometimes we get so caught up in the pressures and seriousness of everyday life that we forget to have a laugh, or even forget how to let go and have a laugh.

What does laughing do?

Below is a list of some of the many benefits of a good laugh:

- Relaxes the body
- Reduces stress
- It's contagious
- Gives a sense of release
- Fills us with happiness and emotional wellbeing
- Brightens our outlook on life
- Improves our health
- Lowers blood pressure
- Connects us with others
- It's a good workout for the stomach muscles

If you and your man can regularly have a laugh together, the benefits this will have for your relationship will be nothing short of astounding.

When was the last time the pair of you had a really good laugh together?

Find ways to make he and yourself laugh (or at the very least smile a lot). Watch some romantic comedies on DVD or at the cinema. A great one is to go see a stand up comedian at your local club. Indulge in a few drinks, loosen up and share a laugh. Tell him a joke when he comes home from work. You can compile a list of endless jokes by searching on the internet. It doesn't matter if the jokes are stupid ones. Sometimes dumb jokes are funny just because they are so stupid.

Does your partner have a good sense of humour?

Hopefully he does.

Find out what makes him laugh (if you don't already know this) and target him with those things. But don't forget about yourself. You need to find it funny too or he'll just be laughing all by himself.

Not that this really matters as we are all aware a good laugh can be highly infectious.

It's a very old and well-used cliché to state that 'laughter is the best medicine'. This saying is one hundred percent true though. That's why they entertain sick children in hospital with clowns and other humorous characters.

Laughter works wonders, so always try and find ways to share a hearty laugh together.

Socialising

As much as quality time to ourselves and alone together as a couple is important, we all need to socialise; to get out amongst others, have some fun and let off some steam.

Some people need this more than others and will require it in larger doses. The amount you wish to socialise or can socialise depends upon your lifestyle, what it is you like to do and how much or how often you can afford to do it.

Even if you and your partner have a busy schedule with work or business, family commitments and everyday chores, always set aside some time to socialise with others.

Maybe you could surprise your man by arranging a dinner party and invite his favourite people along? Or organise some friends to meet up for dinner somewhere and a night on the town. Schedule a barbecue in the local park. Invite some friends and relatives. Everyone can bring food so it will work out pretty cheap. Arrange a few sports to play. Having something to do at a gathering always helps to keep things relaxed and casual with no awkward moments.

Even if time and finances are constrained, at least try to get out and about amongst others at least once a month.

Watching Sport

Men *need* to do this!

I can't stress this enough. We men need our fix of sports. It's a part of our Neanderthal and primeval instincts and is hard-wired into our brains and deeply embedded in our constitution. Without our regular doses of our favourite sports, many of us would become very frustrated individuals indeed.

Of course, not all men are into sports and watching them live at the game or on television, but most of us are. If your partner doesn't like sport – either participating or viewing – then this will never be an issue for you. However, if you are partnered with one of the vast majority of men who do, then his desire to watch sport will be something you have to deal with.

If he watches sports for hours on end, day after day, then this will definitely become a problem for you. And rightly so. This kind of self-absorbed and inconsiderate male will be a total bore. Unless, by some chance you are into sports as much as he is, your quality time together will suffer greatly, if not become totally obsolete.

I'm writing this section under the premise that your man isn't that inconsiderate and utterly dull. If your partner chooses to watch three or four hours a week of his favourite sports, don't complain about it. Just let him be. He'll be grateful for your consideration of his needs. Even surprise him occasionally by encouraging him to watch some sport, or join him and share the experience for an hour or two.

You just might surprise yourself and find that you actually even enjoy it.

Intimacy

Always find time or make time for intimacy in your relationship. Intimacy, as obvious as this statement will be, is what makes you two lovers and not merely just friends.

An entire section will be devoted to this subject later in the book, but I felt it appropriate to make a mention of it now as intimacy definitely comes under the umbrella of quality time.

Around the House

Who does what and when around the house can often become a point of contention among couples. One partner may be more than pulling their weight while the other is slack, which can lead to a degree of bitterness and a sense of unfairness.

Then there is the issue of roles. Does he expect you to clean because you are a woman? Do you expect him to mow the lawn because he is a man?

Inside The Home

Women, by nature, tend to automatically take charge of this zone and want it to be their domain. This doesn't mean that every chore or task that needs to be done inside the house has to be done by, or left to her.

If you both have to work, then the jobs to be done at home will need to be shared. And if they don't get shared, then one of you is bound to get really peeved off.

I used to know this guy once who was married. His wife didn't work, but he did. At the end of each work day he would come home and vacuum the floors, do the washing, clean the house, cook the dinner, bath the kids and put them to bed. During this time his wife would be perched on the couch, a box of chocolates in her lap, remote control in her hand and her eyes glued to the television.

I'll be straight up with you. It is a very rare male indeed who would be willing to endure a situation like that.

Likewise, neither should the reverse be true where the female is lumbered with work and all the home duties as well. It is all about balance.

Obviously if you are both working fulltime he'll need to contribute some effort in keeping the place clean, tidy and up to scratch.

A point that became very evident in the surveys was this: Men find something quite attractive in the way a woman takes charge of the home and its upkeep. A woman who takes pride in keeping the house neat and clean, nicely decorated and laid out, providing a comfortable environment for her man is a highly regarded quality, according to many males.

This is not meant to sound sexist. It's just the way it is.

Outside The House

Often considered the man's domain, and he'll usually enjoy and quite naturally take charge of this area.

Work outside the house just instinctively feels like a more masculine environment to men. I'm not sure if it's the sun on our backs, the open air, the dirt, or what.

Of course women like to get outdoors and work in the garden etcetera too. It's certainly not exclusively a man's realm by any means.

If this is where your man feels most comfortable in doing his share of the chores and domestic duties, then let him have it. However, every now and then it would be a pleasant surprise for him if you did one of his chores for him; especially if he's recently been working extremely hard and was dreading coming home and mowing that lawn or sweeping up those leaves.

Who knows? It could even inspire him to knock over a couple of your chores occasionally when you least expect it.

Cooking

Some men can be great cooks, and a growing number of males are finding enjoyment pottering around in the kitchen and making a meal for two.

That's the catch right there. Men are renowned for not bothering to cook much or eat very healthy meals when on their own. But give them a more valid reason to cook and things can be different.

I don't know what your man is like in preparing culinary delights. Maybe he's so woeful that you feel you will live longer if he never steps foot in the kitchen again. No matter. He can always treat you to a dinner out instead.

We males enjoy being looked after in that way. When a woman prepares a delicious meal for us - and it doesn't have to be extravagant either. I personally will eat just about anything put in front of me - we derive a certain satisfaction from it. Not because we think that it's the woman's place and we get off on seeing her slave away in the kitchen.

It's not that at all.

We respect it. To us it feels like our lady is taking the time out to please us – and our stomachs.

If you have a spacious and well laid out kitchen, preparing a more lavish meal *together* is a great form of quality time, a positive bonding session and can be fun for the both of you.

Your guy may be reluctant to cook. Or he just plain doesn't have the confidence because he doesn't know how. If that's the case, try enticing him to help you prepare his favourite dish. That way, if he is learning to cook the food he most likes to eat, the more he'll be interested in learning and lending a hand.

Just a thought.

The BBQ

Definitely predominantly the man's domain.

We men gravitate to barbecues like the flies do to the steaks we are cooking on them. There has always been some natural appeal for a man to wield a pair of tongs over a greasy open-air grill.

It’s all about that outdoor thing. Men seem to feel most at home and most comfortable doing things outside of the house.

Always let him have his barbecue fun. Even if he burns the sausages, at least he’s enjoying himself and you don’t have to cook for a change.

The Extended
Circle

The extended circle includes all other people who immediately and regularly interact in the lives of you and your partner. It includes family and friends, children, work colleagues, the in-laws, and maybe even an ex-partner.

It is important that you learn to interact with your partner's circle of friends, family and acquaintances, and that you are capable of adaptation and compromise.

Children

Are there children involved in your relationship? If so, are you and your partner the natural parents of the children? Does he have children from a past relationship? Do you perhaps have offspring fathered by a previous lover? Do the children from other partners live with the pair of you?

If neither of you has children, either together or otherwise, then there is nothing to consider; except maybe the possibility of kids in the future. If you have children where the both of you are the biological parents, then you will be in a more natural situation regarding them.

What I plan to touch on in this topic is the subject of children to previous partners and how this may affect your man. The children might be yours from a previous love, or they could be his. Possibly you both have offspring from past encounters and relationships.

When I refer to children I'm talking about kids that aren't yet old enough to live away from their parents.

If his child or children live with you, he may be expecting you to be somewhat of a mother to them. Some women will be quite comfortable with this role while others will not. If you are comfortable with it there will be no real problem. On the other hand, if you are apprehensive about his expecting that of you, then you need to bring this to his attention and explain to him why.

This will be a delicate subject. After all, it's his own flesh and blood. Possibly you will relax in the role over time, but if not, explain to him that you are happy to be their friend and support, but you don't want the mother role.

Another point to consider here - whether his kids live with you or not – is that from time to time you are going to be encountering his ex-partner; the mother of his children.

How well do you deal with that?

If there is no reason for concern and your man gives you no reason to worry, then these occasional encounters won't present an issue (though it will probably always feel a little awkward).

Try to avoid falling into the jealousy trap, hating him having anything to do with her even though he has to for the sake of the children. Feeling that way will do you no favours at all. It will make things very awkward for your partner and just cause friction between the two of you.

If your man and his ex *do* give you genuine reason for concern, then you have every right to make a firm statement about it and bring it to a head. A situation like this would likely be an indicator that your relationship is not doing so well, and that perhaps he's not a man you want to keep after all.

The reverse scenario is if you have kids and he doesn't. Being the mother, chances are high the children live with you and your partner.

Do you expect him to adopt the role of father to them? If so, how does he feel about this? Has he told you? Have you asked him? Do you make sure that he still gets some much needed time out for himself?

In an ideal world you will no doubt hope that he can love your children the same way you do. Some men can do this while others cannot. After all, they are not his own flesh and blood. He didn't play a part in their conception, he wasn't present at the birth, he hasn't known them all their lives and he will never have that same connection with them as you do.

With that all said and done, even if he can't love them like they were his own, that doesn't mean that he doesn't love them at all. It's just a different kind of love; probably more like a brotherly love, or the love one has for a close friend. This kind of love should be enough to satisfy everyone and I don't think it is fair in either scenario for one partner or the other to expect anything more.

If he loves your children like they are his own, then that's an added bonus.

The In-Laws

The two of you don't have to be married to have parents in-law. All couples have 'unofficial' in-laws, and it seems to be quite common for the parents of one partner not to be entirely happy with their son's or daughter's choice in a mate. No one knows exactly why this is. The only logical explanation for this phenomenon is that most parents never feel anyone is quite good enough for their children.

Hopefully you get along famously with your man's parents. Maybe they even love you like their own daughter? That's the best case scenario.

More than likely, though, you will be one of the many who get along with their in-laws, but the in-laws always have some reservations about you.

Obviously the worst case scenario is the one where you don't get along with them at all; perhaps not even associating with them.

Whichever scenario you fall under you will still have to show some degree of respect, however mild. After all, they are his parents.

Through my interviews I discovered a common thread. Even a partner who doesn't particularly like their own parents will still get offended if their mate expresses too much distaste for them.

The 'blood is thicker than water' analogy comes into play.

If things are not great with the in-laws, do your best to be pleasant and get along with them as much as you can manage. If you are really keen to improve the situation, maybe even consider having a one-on-one chat with each in-law in private and work out why they have a problem with you. At the very least they will respect you more for being forthright.

The situation will be pretty much the same in reverse. If your man doesn't get along with your mum and dad, he will still need to show some respect for your sake. If he refuses to do so, talk to him about the reasons why. If nothing can be resolved there, at least plead with him to be civil to them for your benefit.

Siblings

Circumstances will be similar with your partner's siblings to that with the in-laws; although your man's brothers and sisters (if he has any) will generally be easier to get along with than the parents.

Often some great friendships can be forged with a partner's siblings.

If your man gets along well with his brothers and sisters, he will be hoping that you can do the same.

Obviously this won't be totally in your control. It also requires some effort from the siblings as well. Once again, if you are not establishing a positive rapport with his brother or sister, strive to be civil, respectful and pleasant. If at all possible, maybe partake of that particular sibling's company in small doses only.

Some ways to create a rapport.

Show an interest in them, both to your partner and the siblings themselves. Get to know them, find out what they like, what they do, where their interests lie. Invite them over for dinner parties and show them what a great host you can be. Exhibit the qualities that their brother loves you for.

Always keep in mind that siblings can be just as protective of each other as the parents can be.

Work Colleagues

How do you feel about the place where your man works and the people he associates with there?

Does he associate with colleagues outside of work hours?

If a pretty girl works where he does, do you feel threatened by this?

If your man genuinely loves you, is happy, and you have chosen your partner carefully based on his character and not just his looks and personality, then there should be absolutely no reason to feel threatened in any way. A man like this, a happy and contented man, will be loyal.

Have trust and faith in him. Even if you know for certain a woman in the office is quite keen on your man, know that he is happy with you and be confident that he will not respond to her advances. Try to avoid indulging in fits of jealousy, or wrongly accusing him of playing up on you. These acts will ultimately spell death for your relationship. If he does do the wrong thing by you, then he was always going to do it anyway and there would have been nothing you could have done to prevent the inevitable.

You don't want to be with a man who is unfaithful at the first opportunity, is obviously of weak character and not committed to your relationship anyway.

You are better off without this kind of man in your life. This type of man would only do your head in, screw with your emotions and basically always muck you around with his game playing and insincerity.

If his work mates aren't really your thing, then that is something you will just have to endure. But maybe he keeps inviting these annoying people around to your home? Let him know, tactfully, that you are not comfortable with these people and perhaps he would be better served if he met up with them elsewhere; or just leave it all behind at work.

His Mates

Every man has mates; and he should never be expected to stop seeing or give up his friends just because he now has a special woman in his life.

Surveys of men, women and couples revealed that quite a few women expected their men to do just this. Which is a ludicrous notion to even suggest.

Everyone needs friends; particularly those of the same sex. Just because a man has a girl in his life shouldn't mean, doesn't mean and can't mean that he no longer needs or wants his friends.

It's evident that some women feel, or fear, that their man's mates will ultimately lead him astray or coax him into cheating on his girl.

Once again I feel the need to reiterate this point:

If you have chosen your man carefully and he loves you and is happy and contented with you he will not stray.

Possibly your partner has a mate that you just don't get along with, don't feel comfortable being around, or that you just plain don't like.

What do you do then?

If the guy is just someone your partner has been recently hanging out with, chances are you will be able to express to your man that you don't feel comfortable with his friend, and don't feel good about your partner having him as a mate. Explain to him why you have reservations and your man may quite readily end the association with this guy.

However, if the person in question is a long-time friend of your partner, a mate he's known for years, much longer than he's known you for (perhaps even a life-long buddy), then the situation will be an entirely different one.

It would be a very big ask to expect your man, now that he's found love with you, to ditch one of his long-term best friends just because you don't happen to like him.

In this instance you will have to tread very carefully. Don't complain to him about his friend in some emotional outburst or demand that he doesn't see him anymore. Doing something like that will go against you big time. The man is obviously a close friend of your partner and that is not likely to change.

The only real option open to you in this case is to talk about your concerns calmly with your man and gently explain to him why you feel uncomfortable, and why you have issues with his mate. If approached tactfully, and if the mate is as sincere about the friendship with your man as your partner is, your guy may decide to chat with his buddy about what he's doing to upset you and hopefully the guy will pull himself into line and the two of you can get along.

You have a specific role to play here too, though. You can't just treat the guy in question poorly, just because you don't want him around. As hard as it may be, you have to play your part in doing your best to get along with him. If you can demonstrate that you are, then your man will be more likely to respond favourably to your concerns and sort out the problems with his friend.

Your Girlfriends

Similar situations can occur for your partner in regards to *your* friends. You might have a girlfriend that he thinks is a complete bitch or something, and the two just don't hit it off. She might be a long-term friend of yours, someone with whom you are not likely to cut ties with.

Ultimately, in that case, she and your partner will have to try to get along to some degree in order for both your relationship with your friend, and your partner, to not be unduly affected.

Gather information from both parties in order to define the problems. Once you are more informed you will then have to sit down with each of them in turn and work out ways to smooth things over so everyone can get along. How you will do that will depend on what the actual issues are. Be objective, hear both sides of the debate, then try to work with your girlfriend and your partner on possible solutions.

A different circumstance would be (and this applies to your partner's mates as well) that perhaps you have a long-term friend who really is just a bad influence on you and you've never realised it until now.

In this case you may be better served to end the relationship with this particular 'so-called' friend – a friend who obviously doesn't have your best interests at heart – in order not to sabotage things with your partner.

Finances

Finances and money play a vital role in all our lives. Not one of us can live in the modern world without a certain amount of it. The subject of money is often a contentious one when it comes to relationships. The lack of income, or the poor handling of it, can create extreme pressures. So often money problems can be the root cause of many a broken marriage and relationship.

In this section I won't be offering financial advice. For that you would be far better served dealing with an expert in the field. What I will be touching on briefly is more the attitude to money and how it will affect your relationship.

Attitude To Money

What is your attitude to money?

Is it the most important component of your relationship?

Does your man live for money?

Is everything in your relationship governed by it and affected by it?

If you answered 'yes' to the last three questions, then your relationship is built upon a foundation that could so very easily crumble.

What happens if the money supply dwindles or income levels drop? Will you instantly be off looking for greener pastures? Will your man cash in his chips and make a run for it?

If either you or your partner entered into the relationship purely for monetary gain, then there was no use at all in even reading this book. Therefore, I am assuming that no woman taking the time to read this book is with their partner purely for money. But that doesn't mean that money doesn't have too big an influence in your relationship.

If it does, you (and your man for that matter) need to rethink what's important to you both; as individuals and especially as a couple. There is nothing wrong with wanting money and having a great lifestyle, and we all need cash to live, but money can't be, can never be, the foundation upon which your entire relationship hinges. Couples need to be able to endure tough times as well as the good and prosperous if they are to survive together. Relationships are primarily about finding a life partner; someone to share your life with.

- Love
- Loyalty
- Commitment
- Lust/Passion
- Romance
- Trust
- Personality/Character

All the things mentioned above should hold more importance than the dollar. They are what your relationship should be built on in order to endure and survive.

Really, when you break it all down, money is simply something we want and need whether we are in a relationship or not. But a relationship requires a whole lot more than money could ever buy.

His Job Status

Even though the world and its attitudes has changed dramatically in recent decades, there still exists the expectation that men are supposed to be the money makers, the bread winners. This belief continues to flow through modern day relationships as well.

Sure, many women today enjoy jobs and careers in the

workforce, and most family budgets are supplemented through incomes brought in by both partners. However, a man is still frequently judged and measured by what sort of job, career or business he has and how much money he brings in each year.

Women want their man to be something, to be a somebody; and often this is directly associated with and pinned to the job he has.

Let me stress at this point that we men understand this and are fine with it.....To a point.

What men *don't* like is undue pressure being placed on them, especially by their partner, to be something they either don't want to be or simply are not cut out to be.

Say you meet your partner and his name is Bob (for the sake of this example). Bob paints houses for a living. He loves painting, is happy with the wage he gets from his boss, and one day hopes to start his own painting business. Bob always wants to be a painter. It suits him. He's happy.

You've met Bob, fallen in love with him, maybe even married him. You knew Bob is a painter and that he always wants to be a painter.

Now, for you to then tell Bob somewhere down the track that he should do something else, something 'better' in your eyes, something that perhaps brings in more money, is an unfair request or demand.

Bob never said that down the line he wants to be something else. He said he always wants to be a painter.

The point being, if you were not happy being with Bob the painter, or the income level his job provides, why did you even decide to go out with Bob? You should have waited to meet a man who suits your needs and desires more appropriately.

Men need to feel that you are supportive of them and happy with what they've chosen to do.

It's a totally different story if your man has always been open to change and new opportunities. If he's always said that he's going to be in his own business one day, or do a course in something and get a better job, then you have every right to ask this of him as time progresses.

Still, you need wisdom and tact here. A little bit of pressure applied here and there works far more effectively than a lot of pressure all at once. Apply too much pressure to anything and what happens? It breaks. Your man will likely snap and probably go off in a totally different direction just to spite you.

If he's still wanting to do other things, or do more with his life but is struggling for a little motivation to take the next step, just prod him here and there but never hound him.

The worst case scenario for you is to be with a man who hates what he currently does for a living, has no idea what he really wants to do or should do, has no solid direction, and not much money or opportunity to try new things and seek out opportunities.

It could be that there is no hope with this man. He may always be directionless, living his life on total chance and pot luck that something falls into his lap.

However, if he has the right attitude, but just needs some encouragement to find a firm direction, then there is hope.

I personally know this because I've been that man.

He's not alone. You are there by his side. You both have a brain. Two heads are better than one. If together you have patience and remain committed, in time you will both help him on his journey in the right direction.

Income

Is there stress in your household that is a result of a lack of money coming in? Do you lay blame on your man? Does he point the finger at you?

Money worries and the ensuing arguments they create are unfortunately a very common occurrence in many relationships.

We need money to survive, we require a certain amount of it to fund our entertainment and socialising, and when there is not enough of it to meet our needs, the pressure builds until eventually it explodes.

I'm not going to enlighten you as to how to generate more money. There are experts in this field who will be much more adept at helping you in that department than I could.

Instead, I'm more concerned with how you and your partner react to each other because of your financial situation.

It's been said before many times over by many different people, but the saying is true: You need to stop bickering, take a deep breath, relax and look at what you *do* have together rather than focusing on what you *don't* have.

Only then will you both be able to think clearly and productively about how to improve your financial situation.

Positive thinking leads to positive actions and results.

Expenses

If only one of you brings in an income then there is no question or confusion about whose money is paying for what.

These days both partners usually bring home an income. So that there are no arguments or uncertainty, have you and your partner mapped out a budget with your combined incomes? Have you worked out whose wage covers what bills and when?

If this is not clearly defined, it may lead to bills not getting paid on time, which then leads to stress followed by conflict.

Maybe one of you is bad with managing money? If that's true, then the best idea is to give the responsibility of all the money and the paying of the bills to the partner in the relationship who is better at managing finances and spending.

If you are both equally as bad at managing money, then it's time to call in that financial advisor.

Another point I would like to address here is one that popped up regularly in the surveys and interviews.

As stated earlier many couples have dual incomes. An irksome point that arose with quite a few men was that even though both partners were bringing home a wage, their girlfriend or wife was still expecting him to pay for just about everything.

If both partners in a relationship are both earning an income, then both have the responsibility to contribute to the running of the home, daily expenses and entertainment. Obviously if one partner is bringing in much more money than the other, then they are going to be contributing more because they can. But both should contribute.

Working Together

If you plan on working together or to run a business together, then you better make sure that you have a very stable, strong and happy relationship before you do.

This needs to be thought about and planned very carefully indeed; not just the business side of things, but more importantly the personal aspects of how it will affect the two of you and what impact it might have on your relationship.

Working together or being in business together can kill a romance and a relationship quicker than just about anything else.

Intimacy

Physical attraction between a man and a woman is a mysterious, intangible something that has always been very hard to explain and define. It goes well beyond thinking a woman is pretty or a guy is handsome. A person's looks are only a part of it.

What attracts you to one person and not another, even though both may be attractive looking?

I'm not going to delve deeply into the mystery of physical attraction. But physical attraction is the necessary element that creates and leads to intimacy.

This section of the book was not left until last because it is the least important. Far from it. True intimacy and keeping the fires of passion alive depend very heavily on other factors in the relationship being in order. If there is friction and discontent between a couple, intimacy is usually the first to suffer.

Physical Appearance

Physical appearance is important; not just to men, but to women as well. We don't all have to be stunningly beautiful or devilishly handsome to be found attractive, but there definitely has to be something there for someone to find us appealing.

You were obviously very attracted to the man in your life or you wouldn't be with him, or desired to be with him in the first place. He might naturally be a hot looking guy, or his features could be considered quite average. But there was obviously something that appealed to you about him physically to attract you to him. A combination of his looks and personality perhaps. An air of quiet confidence. Many things can contribute to making us physically appealing.

The same goes for your man with you. He felt drawn to you from the start. You projected a magnetism that lured him in.

Hopefully both you and your man still find each other very physically appealing. You have to in order for intimacy to happen and be fulfilling.

If either of you (or the both of you) is not feeling sufficiently attracted to the other – or attracted as much – you need to work out the reasons why.

Other factors in the relationship might be struggling, therefore stifling your ability to find your partner attractive. These areas need to be identified and rectified.

Or maybe you just aren't keeping yourself as attractive looking as you once did?

Don't Let Yourself Go

You always want your man to think you *look hot*. And he will if you don't let yourself go.

Letting yourself go to flab or generally no longer caring about how you look will turn your man off as quickly as anything can. And it's not just the end result of this that will do it either.

It is the attitude behind it!

This tells him one thing: You have him now and you no longer need (or want) to put in any effort to keep him.

Wrong.

The secret is this: It's not all about how you look. It's about how much you care about how you look for him.

We all age. Lines start to appear on the face. Our bodies struggle against a fading metabolism and the forces of gravity. We slowly lose the battle against time and we never look as good as we once did in our youth.

But this is not letting ourselves go. This is the natural ageing process.

Letting yourself go means to not care about how you look, or do your best to look your best. The very fact that you are trying to look after yourself and your appearance, and not letting yourself go, is something that men find *extremely* attractive in a woman.

You should always try to keep fit and in the best possible shape you can be. Encourage your man to do the same. After all, you both want to remain attractive to the other, not just one of you.

Keep your hair nice. Whether it's long or shorter doesn't really matter. It's all about what suits you and your look, and what appeals to him. Try a few different colours sometimes. It keeps things interesting.

Most women like to wear some degree of makeup. Don't overdo it. Wear some at home occasionally. Don't just save it for when you are off to work or going out someplace. Doing that suggests that you don't really care what you look like for him, just everybody else. Your man is the one you should care the most about impressing.

Likewise, do you dress nicely when out and about, but always save your most daggy clothing for around the house? This is fine to a point. After all, you want to be comfortable. But don't always dress your worst whilst at home. Sure, wear some comfortable clothes, but also don some clothing that shows you off to your man. Maybe even parade around in some lingerie occasionally? Imagine his surprise to come home from work one day to see you in the kitchen preparing his favourite meal dressed in a slinky negligee.

You would win him over in a split second and have him down on his knees.

Don't forget to be sensual around the home. It not only suggests the possibility of intimate moments, but it also imparts an air of spice and excitement to the ambience.

Personal Hygiene

Poor personal hygiene is a major turn off for both men and women alike.

I'm not suggesting for one minute that you or your partner suffer from this. I'm just making the point that maintaining good hygiene is very important for intimacy and it's enjoyment.

Keeping certain areas of the body neatly trimmed and groomed certainly aids in this, as do the more obvious ones of bathing regularly, brushing the teeth, deodorant and general grooming.

Always maintain high levels of personal hygiene. And if your partner slackens off in this area, give him some encouragement by enticing him with promises of what you will do to him if he looks after himself.

Affection

Affection is independent of sex, but is still also a part of it and associated with it.

Acts of affection toward our partner show that we care about them, need them, love them and support them. It also demonstrates that we are attracted to them.

A positive and truly fulfilling relationship should have, and needs loads of, fondness and affectionate interaction between you and your man.

Some people are naturally more affectionate than others. Maybe due to upbringing? Who knows for sure? But everyone is capable of affection if coupled with the right partner.

We all know what acts of affection are.

- Kissing and cuddling
- Holding hands
- Walking arm in arm
- A caring or reassuring touch
- Words of endearment
- Saying "I love you"

Affection helps to keep a couple close. It makes each partner feel special to the other.

Always strive to keep affection well and truly alive in your relationship. Encourage your man to show affection – both in private and in public – by being openly affectionate towards him.

Romance

Romance is an essential ingredient for a successful relationship. It creates:

- Love
- Affection
- Excitement
- Euphoria
- Lust
- Passion
- Intimacy
- Feeling alive

Never let the romance between you and your man fade away and die. This tragically happens to many couples. When romance doesn't exist, affection can diminish and sex can become routine and boring (if it doesn't totally cease altogether).

But it doesn't have to be that way.

Many women rely on the man to be the romantic one; the instigator. Don't wait for your man to do it, don't be totally dependent on him. You are just as capable, if not more so, of being romantic as he is. Sure, you want your guy to perform acts of romance without you prompting him. We all want that. But that should never stop you from performing your own romantic acts.

Positive acts are always infectious. All it takes is one person to have the initiative to make the first move.

We spoke earlier in the book about making sure you and your

partner have quality time together. That also includes romantic moments. That night out of town spent in a motel written about earlier is a great opportunity for you to promote romance in your relationship.

I assure you, for every way you are romantic to your man, he will return the favour ten fold. It's all about encouragement and putting romance out there so it is continually on both of your minds.

Ways to be romantic will come naturally to the both of you. Once it's in the air it will flow effortlessly through your relationship like melted chocolate.

Sex

From a male point of view I can sum this up in three words:

Men need it.

We men didn't design our bodies and our brains. We are just the way we've been created to be.

Now, I'm not suggesting that women don't need sex too. Of course women do. We all do. Not just because it's enjoyable. We all have hormones racing through our bodies, a build up of sexual tensions and we all need that release that comes with sex on a regular basis.

Men are often criticised for always wanting sex, or even being somewhat sexually demanding on occasion. That is only because we really physically need it. It's not due to the fact that sex is all we want and care about, or all that we are interested in.

A great sex life catapults your relationship into a higher realm. It makes you closer than ever as a couple. There is no greater joy in life than a loving couple having great sex together on a regular basis.

We should all be in this position: Having a great partner and a fantastic sex life with that partner.

It's true that the day to day rigours of life can take the shine off our sex lives. But only if we allow it. If we strive to keep our relationships balanced and healthy, show genuine affection, find time for romance, then there is no logical reason why we can't indulge in euphoric and greatly satisfying sex together.

Stoking The Fires of Passion

Don't always wait for your man to initiate sex. And don't always turn down his advances as if it's something you hate doing, or have to perform out of duty.

This is the man you love.

Enjoy him!

You are in a relationship now. There is no need to play hard to get – except for the fun of it.

Let yourself go completely and totally give yourself to your partner. Lose all inhibitions. They only serve to stifle the enjoyment and detract from the spontaneity.

If you are performing oral acts (and his personal hygiene is good), take pleasure in it. Relish it. The more you genuinely enjoy giving him pleasure the more he will enjoy it, and the more likely he will enthusiastically return the favour.

Look for ways to create variety. Change positions. Try new locations. Do it out in the open somewhere. Don't always restrict it to the bedroom. Wear that sexy lingerie. Entice him to wear something that you find a turn on.

Be vocal during sex. Encourage him to do the things you like by verbally letting him know how much you are enjoying yourself.

Never ever let the fire go out. Always search for ways to stoke the fires of passion and keep them burning in your relationship forever.

Fidelity and Faithfulness

Fidelity and faithfulness are very much one and the same thing and always go hand in hand.

Basically they mean to be loyal and to never cheat on your

partner.

You've searched long and hard to find the right man, to attract him to you, and to do all the right things to keep him. He now loves you, is happy and contented, and never wants to be with another woman ever again.

He's doing all the right things to fulfill your needs, to keep you happy and you love him. You are contented.

There is never any excuse for cheating on one's partner, and if you are both truly happy, neither of you ever will.

If the relationship is that bad that one or both partners find themselves attracted to someone outside of the relationship, then that relationship should be ended first *before* anything like this takes place. To remain in a relationship whilst playing around on the side is an act of pure selfishness; and selfishness has no part in a truly loving and openly caring relationship

Once again I stress, there is never, ever any valid excuse for cheating by either partner.

In Conclusion

This book has not covered every possible scenario or problem that a relationship can encounter. It has been a heartfelt endeavour to highlight some of the things a woman can do (and a man too, for that matter) to improve her life with her man and keep him and herself happy, contented and *together*.

If the advice offered in this book is followed, and you have truly chosen a compatible partner with which to share your life, then there is every chance that your relationship with your man will be a positively rewarding experience, and one that will endure for a lifetime.

I wish you all true happiness!

Made in the USA
Lexington, KY
05 June 2015